And others, Crispus Attucks

A memorial of Crispus Attucks, Samuel Maverick, James Caldwell, Samuel Gray, and Patrick Carr

From the City of Boston

And others, Crispus Attucks

A memorial of Crispus Attucks, Samuel Maverick, James Caldwell, Samuel Gray, and Patrick Carr
From the City of Boston

ISBN/EAN: 9783337058401

Printed in Europe, USA, Canada, Australia, Japan

Cover: Foto ©ninafisch / pixelio.de

More available books at **www.hansebooks.com**

A

MEMORIAL

OF

CRISPUS ATTUCKS, SAMUEL MAVERICK JAMES CALDWELL, SAMUEL GRAY AND PATRICK CARR

FROM THE

CITY OF BOSTON

[The Boston Massacre, March 5, 1770, may be regarded as the first act in the drama of the American Revolution. "From that moment," said Daniel Webster, "we may date the severance of the British Empire." The presence of the British soldiers in King street excited the patriotic indignation of the people. . . . Led by Crispus Attucks, the mulatto slave, and shouting, "The way to get rid of these soldiers is to attack the main guard; strike at the root! this is the nest!" with more valor than discretion they rushed to King street, and were fired upon by Captain Preston's company. Crispus Attucks was the first to fall; he and Samuel Gray and James Caldwell were killed on the spot. Samuel Maverick and Patrick Carr were mortally wounded. — *Historical Research*, by *George Livermore*. — *Mass. Hist. Society*.]

BOSTON
PRINTED BY ORDER OF THE CITY COUNCIL
1889

CITY OF BOSTON.

IN BOARD OF ALDERMEN, November 26, 1888.

Ordered, That the Clerk of Committees be authorized to prepare for publication, under the direction of the Committee on Printing, an account of the proceedings at the dedication of the Crispus Attucks Monument, and that the said Committee have the volume printed as a city publication, the expense incurred thereby to be charged to the appropriation for printing.

Passed.

Sent down for concurrence.

December 13, came up concurred.

Approved by the Mayor December 17, 1888.

A true copy.

Attest:

JOHN T. PRIEST,
Assistant City Clerk.

CONTENTS.

	PAGE
ACTION OF THE COMMONWEALTH OF MASSACHUSETTS	11
ACTION OF THE CITY OF BOSTON	19
DESCRIPTION OF THE MONUMENT	27
UNVEILING THE MONUMENT ON BOSTON COMMON	31
Prayer by Rev. Eli Smith	33
Remarks of William H. Dupree	36
Remarks of Governor Oliver Ames	38
Remarks of Mayor Hugh O'Brien	39
EXERCISES AT FANEUIL HALL	43
Prayer by Rev. Albert H. Plumb	43
Remarks of Governor Oliver Ames	46
Remarks of Mayor Hugh O'Brien	46
Poem by John Boyle O'Reilly	51
Address by Mr. John Fiske	59
LETTERS	93
Frederick Douglass	93
Dr. Henry I. Bowditch	95
Rev. Phillips Brooks, D.D.	96
Rev. David Gregg	96
Hon. John M. Langston	96

ACTION OF THE COMMONWEALTH OF

ACTION OF THE COMMONWEALTH OF MASSACHUSETTS.

In the spring of 1887 the following petition was presented to the Legislature : —

To the Honorable Senate and House of Representatives of the Commonwealth of Massachusetts, in General Court assembled: —

The undersigned petitioners, citizens of the Commonwealth of Massachusetts, respectfully represent

That in the Granary Burial Ground, in Boston, rest the remains of Crispus Attucks, Samuel Gray, Jonas Caldwell, and Samuel Maverick, who, together with Patrick Carr, led by Crispus Attucks, were the first Martyrs in the cause of American Liberty, having been shot by the British soldiers on the night of the fifth of March, A.D. 1770, known as the Boston Massacre. Their names appear on the records and history of that time, but no stone marks their burial-place.

We, therefore, respectfully request that a suitable monument may be erected to the memory of these early patriots of the Revolution.

And, as in duty bound, will ever pray, etc.

Lewis Hayden,
A. H. Grimké,
Henry J. Gardner,
N. P. Banks,
Wm. Claflin,
Wm. B. Washburn,
William Gaston,
Alexander H. Rice,
John D. Long,
Benjamin F. Butler,
George D. Robinson,
Henry B. Peirce,
Henry Cabot Lodge,
Leopold Morse,
John E. Russell,
Patrick A. Collins,

John F. Andrew,
A. W. Beard,
Hugh O'Brien,
Wm. H. Dupree,
John Boyle O'Reilly,
Butler R. Wilson,
E. B. Haskell,
John Q. Adams,
Charles R. Ladd,
Henry J. Wells,
Charles R. Codman,
George W. Lowther,
Abner C. Goodell, Jr.,
Dr. Henry I. Bowditch,
Rev. Phillips Brooks, D.D.,

W. W. Blackmar,
Martin Brimmer,
Carroll D. Wright,
F. A. Walker,
R. P. Hallowell,
M. P. Kennard,
A. E. Pillsbury,
Harris C. Hartwell,
Roland Worthington,
Charles L. Mitchell,
C. B. Tillinghast,
William H. Jarvis,
Rev. J. T. Jenifer, D.D.,
Thomas P. Taylor,
John H. Lewis,
John J. Smith,

And many other well-known citizens of the State.

As a result thereof the following resolve was adopted without opposition in either house, and was promptly signed by His Excellency, Gov. OLIVER AMES: —

[CHAPTER 53.]

Commonwealth of Massachusetts.

In the Year One Thousand Eight Hundred and Eighty-Seven.

RESOLVE PROVIDING FOR THE ERECTION OF A MEMORIAL TO CRISPUS ATTUCKS, SAMUEL GRAY, JONAS CALDWELL, SAMUEL MAVERICK, AND PATRICK CARR.

Resolved, That the Governor and Council be and they are hereby authorized and requested to cause to be erected in some public place in the city of Boston a suitable memorial or monument to the memory of Crispus Attucks, Samuel Gray, Jonas Caldwell, Samuel Maverick, and Patrick Carr, who were killed by British soldiers in the streets of Boston, on the fifth day of March, in the year seventeen hundred and seventy, upon the occasion known as the "Boston Massacre;" also to cause suitable headstones to be placed at the graves of the said persons, where their locations can be ascertained. The amount to be expended under this resolve shall not exceed the sum of ten thousand dollars.

HOUSE OF REPRESENTATIVES, May 6, 1887. Passed.

CHAS. J. NOYES, *Speaker*.

IN SENATE, May 11, 1887. Passed.

HALSEY J. BOARDMAN, *President*.

MAY 17, 1887. Approved.

OLIVER AMES.

SECRETARY'S DEPARTMENT, BOSTON, NOV. 28, 1888.
A true copy.

Witness the Seal of the Commonwealth.

HENRY B. PEIRCE,
Secretary of the Commonwealth.

[CHAPTER 16.]

Commonwealth of Massachusetts.

In the Year One Thousand Eight Hundred and Eighty-Eight.

RESOLVE CONCERNING THE ERECTION OF A MEMORIAL TO CRISPUS ATTUCKS AND OTHERS.

Resolved, That Chapter fifty-three of the Resolves of the year eighteen hundred and eighty-seven be and hereby is amended by striking out the word "Jonas," and inserting in place thereof the word "James," so that it shall read James Caldwell instead of Jonas Caldwell.

HOUSE OF REPRESENTATIVES, Feb. 17, 1888. Passed.
                              CHAS. J. NOYES, *Speaker.*

IN SENATE, Feb. 20, 1888. Passed.
                              HALSEY J. BOARDMAN, *President.*

FEB. 21, 1888. Approved.
                              OLIVER AMES.

SECRETARY'S DEPARTMENT, BOSTON, NOV. 28, 1888.
A true copy.
       Witness the Seal of the Commonwealth.
                              HENRY B. PEIRCE,
                              Secretary of the Commonwealth.

From a number of designs submitted, the Governor and Council selected that one made by Mr. ROBERT KRAUS, and the contract was awarded to him by the following order: —

COMMONWEALTH OF MASSACHUSETTS,
COUNCIL CHAMBER, BOSTON, July 27, 1888.

Ordered, That the design submitted by Robert Kraus, for a memorial to be erected to the memory of Crispus Attucks, Samuel Gray, Jonas Caldwell, Samuel Maverick, and Patrick Carr, as provided in Resolve, Chapter 53, of 1887, be approved; provided, that there shall be no outlay on the part of the Commonwealth until a contract shall have been duly executed, insuring the completion of the work contemplated by said resolve, including suitable headstones, at an expense not exceeding ten thousand dollars.

Adopted.

HENRY B. PEIRCE, *Secretary.*

SECRETARY'S DEPARTMENT, BOSTON, Nov. 28, 1888.

A true copy.

HENRY B. PEIRCE,
Secretary of the Commonwealth.

On the fifth day of September, His Excellency the Governor sent the following letter to a number of public-spirited gentlemen: —

COMMONWEALTH OF MASSACHUSETTS,
EXECUTIVE DEPARTMENT.

DEAR SIR, — At some date in the near future, which is to be fixed, the monument in commemoration of Crispus Attucks and others, who were victims of the Boston Massacre, is to be placed by the Commonwealth on Boston Common. Under the terms of the resolve providing for the erection of this memorial, there is no provision for anything beyond the cost of its being constructed.

It is thought by many that its unveiling should be marked by some demonstration; and in order that this may take place, the public must be so interested in the matter as to provide for it sufficient funds.

ACTION OF THE COMMONWEALTH.

I take the liberty of suggesting to you that you confer a favor upon all the people of the Commonwealth if you will become one of a voluntary committee, whose duty it shall be to arrange for an appropriate dedication of the monument, such arrangement to include the collection and disbursement of the money which may be needed to carry out the plan that may be determined upon by those who will form the committee.

I am yours very respectfully,

OLIVER AMES,
Governor.

In response to the above letter, the following gentlemen met at the State House, and organized a committee to make arrangements for the unveiling and dedication of the monument: —

Lewis Hayden,	Chas. L. Mitchell,
Rev. Chas. L. Woodworth, D.D.,	John H. Lewis,
William O. Armstrong,	D. Toy,
John Boyle O'Reilly,	A. H. Grimké,
John J. Smith,	John J. Teevens,
John A. Daly,	Wm. Power Wilson,
J. C. Chappelle,	N. G. Gaskins,
John Patten,	Dr. Henry I. Bowditch,
Wm. H. Dupree,	Butler R. Wilson,

E. M. Chamberlin.

Mr. William H. Dupree was made chairman, and Butler R. Wilson and Edwin M. Chamberlin were made secretaries.

The committee invited Mr. John Fiske, of Cambridge, to deliver the historical address, and Mr. John Boyle O'Reilly to write a poem. Both invitations were accepted, and the 14th of November was selected as the day upon which the services were to be held.

Faneuil Hall was secured, and for the better accommodation of the military and civic organizations invited to take part in a parade preceding the exercises, a thousand seats were placed on the floor of the hall, and the gallery was reserved for special guests holding tickets.

Among those invited by the committee on behalf of the Commonwealth were the following: His Excellency the Governor, the Executive Council, the Senators and Representatives of Massachusetts in Congress, United States civil officers in Boston, the judges of the Supreme and Superior Courts, the heads of State Departments, the members of the General Court, the Mayor of Boston, the Board of Aldermen, the senior member from each ward of the Common Council, and representatives of the Press.

ACTION OF THE CITY GOVERNMENT.

ACTION OF THE CITY GOVERNMENT.

In his inaugural address, His Honor Mayor O'Brien referred to the fact that the Crispus Attucks Monument, for which the State had appropriated the sum of ten thousand dollars, was nearly completed, and he recommended that a location be provided for the monument on Boston Common, in accordance with the desire of the Governor and Committee in charge. The matter was referred to the Joint Standing Committee on Common and Public Grounds. Subsequently, on the 28th of August, a message on the subject was received by the Board of Aldermen from His Honor the Mayor, covering a communication from His Excellency Governor Ames, as follows: —

CITY OF BOSTON,
EXECUTIVE DEPARTMENT, Aug. 20, 1888.

To the Honorable the City Council: —

GENTLEMEN, — The monument to Crispus Attucks will be completed in about six weeks. The City Council last year appropriated two thousand dollars for a foundation from the Phillips fund. It will be necessary to commence work immediately on the foundation, but the location of the monument has not yet been fixed by the City Council.

His Excellency Governor Ames, whose communication is herewith submitted, has made a selection near the West-street gate of the Common, and I hope you will give it your favorable consideration.

Respectfully submitted,

HUGH O'BRIEN,
Mayor.

COMMONWEALTH OF MASSACHUSETTS.
EXECUTIVE DEPARTMENT, BOSTON, Nov. 2, 1887.

His Honor MAYOR HUGH O'BRIEN: —

DEAR SIR, — I have your favor of the 1st inst., in which you say that it appears to you that I "have the sole right to place the Attucks Monument."

If such be the case, I would select for the position on which to place that memorial a spot on the Common, just south of the West-street gate, between the Tremont-street mall and the mall from West street to Park square, nearly on a line with the store on the east side of Tremont street which is occupied by Messrs. Hallet & Cumston.

Thanking you heartily for the privilege which you have in this matter accorded me,

I am yours sincerely,

OLIVER AMES,
Governor.

These communications were in like manner referred to the Committee on Common and Public Grounds.

As it was discovered that there were serious objections to locating the monument upon the site selected, from the fact that the foundation would come in contact with the water-pipes laid through the Common, the matter was brought to the Governor's attention, and a new site was selected at a point southerly of that first selected, and information to that effect was communicated to the City Council on October 1, by the following messages from His Honor the Mayor, namely : —

CITY OF BOSTON,
EXECUTIVE DEPARTMENT, Oct. 1, 1888.

To the Honorable the City Council: —

GENTLEMEN, — I enclose herewith a communication from His Excellency the Governor concerning the site for the monument to

Crispus Attucks. It will be observed by the plan which accompanies the communication that the Governor has chosen a spot for the site close by the one formerly selected by him. As the work is far advanced, and the city is ready to put in the foundation, so that the dedication of the monument can take place the present month, it is very desirable that the City Council promptly ratify the action taken by the Governor.

Yours respectfully,
HUGH O'BRIEN,
Mayor.

COMMONWEALTH OF MASSACHUSETTS,
EXECUTIVE DEPARTMENT, BOSTON, Sept. 27, 1888.

DEAR MR. MAYOR,— Because of the representation to me that to place the Attucks Monument on the site first selected by me would be attended by certain difficulties which will not be insurmountable, but will be inconvenient, I have this day visited the Common, and have decided that the monument shall be placed in the same plot of land, but southerly of the place first chosen, very nearly at the point which corresponds to that marked with the figures "85" on the enclosed plan, and opposite the store on Tremont street occupied by the White Sewing Machine Company.

I am yours sincerely,
OLIVER AMES.

HON. HUGH O'BRIEN, *Mayor of Boston.*

The message was referred to the Committee on Common and Public Grounds.

In connection with the above, Alderman Wilson offered the following: —

Ordered, That His Honor the Mayor be authorized to expend in behalf of the city a sum not exceeding one thousand dollars in connection with the arrangements for dedicating the Crispus Attucks Monument on Boston Common; said sum to be charged to the appropriation for incidentals.

The order was passed by both branches of the City Council, and approved by the Mayor October 13.

On the 18th of October a report was received in the Board of Aldermen from the Committee on Common and Public Grounds, recommending the passage of the following order, namely: —

Ordered, That the site selected by His Excellency the Governor for the location of the Crispus Attucks Monument on Boston Common be hereby approved.

Report accepted, order passed under a suspension of the rule. Sent down.

The order was passed by the Common Council in concurrence, and approved by the Mayor October 13.

On the 19th of November the following message was received in the Board of Aldermen from His Honor the Mayor in relation to publishing a memorial volume, containing an account of the proceedings at the dedication of the monument, namely: —

CITY OF BOSTON,
EXECUTIVE DEPARTMENT, Nov. 19, 1888.

To the Honorable the City Council: —

GENTLEMEN, — The dedication of the monument to Crispus Attucks, in which the State and the city participated, was quite a memorable event in the history of Boston. I therefore recommend that a memorial volume be printed, containing the addresses and proceedings on that occasion.

Respectfully submitted,

HUGH O'BRIEN,
Mayor.

The message was referred to the Joint Standing Committee on Printing, and on the 26th of November the committee reported the order, which was adopted, and which prefaces this volume.

DESCRIPTION OF THE MONUMENT.

DESCRIPTION OF THE MONUMENT.

The Monument is of Concord granite, twenty-five feet six inches high, and measures ten feet six inches at the base. The pedestal, which is round, except where a rectangular projection is made to support the statue and receive the relief, is eight feet two inches high. The bas-relief on the face of the pedestal represents the Boston Massacre in King street. In the foreground lies Crispus Attucks, the first victim of British bullets; the centre of the scene is the old State House, behind which may be seen the steeple of the old brick or First church, which stood on Cornhill, now Washington street. In the upper left-hand corner is the following inscription: "From that Moment we may date the Severance of the British Empire. Daniel Webster;" and in the upper right-hand corner, "On that Night the Foundation of American Independence was laid. John Adams." Under the relief on the base appears the date, "March 5, 1770." Above the bas-relief stands "Free America." With her left hand she clasps a flag about to be unfurled, while she holds aloft in her right hand the broken chain of oppression, and crushes beneath her right foot the royal crown, which, twisted and torn, is falling off the plinth. At her left side, clinging to the edge of the plinth, is an eagle. Its wings are raised, its beak is open, and it has apparently just lit. Its pose is in unison with the fiery spirit of its mistress, shown in the serious, determined, and heroic gaze of her upturned face.

The statue is seven feet high, and weighs one thousand seven hundred and ninety pounds. Beneath the apex of the shaft, cut into the surface, are thirteen stars, which suggest the original thirteen States of the Union. Below the stars in raised letters appear the names of Crispus Attucks, Samuel Gray, James Caldwell, Samuel Maverick, and Patrick Carr, the five victims of the massacre.

UNVEILING THE MONUMENT ON BOSTON COMMON.

UNVEILING THE MONUMENT ON BOSTON COMMON.

The day set apart for the unveiling and dedication of the monument was a most delightful one. Better weather could not have been chosen.

Promptly at 11 o'clock A.M. the procession of military and civic organizations moved from the corner of Beacon and Charles streets to the State House, where the Governor and other guests were received in escort. It then moved down Beacon and School streets to the City Hall, where the Mayor and representatives of the City Government were received. Thence it marched through School, Washington, and Boylston streets, and entered the Common at the Park-square entrance, and then proceeded through the Boylston and Tremont street malls to the site of the monument — which stands in the centre of a triangular lot facing Tremont street — in the following order: —

Detachment of Mounted Police.

CHIEF MARSHAL.
Major Frederick B. Bogan.

CHIEF OF STAFF.
Capt. C. F. A. Francis.

AIDS.

George Sparrow,	Joseph Lee,
Robert J. Taylor,	Nelson T. Wentworth,

Lieut. W. H. McCafferty,   Daniel Hayes,
Dr. T. O'Donnell,   W. J. Williams,
Charles Johnson,   Charles E. Harris.

Germania Band, 32 men.
Company L, 6th Regiment, M.V.M.,
Capt. George W. Brady, commander, 55 men,
with staff, consisting of
Adjutant W. S. Butler,
Quartermaster Summers,
Paymaster George W. Lowther,
Lieutenant Bell.
Second Separate Company Rhode Island Militia,
Capt. J. E. Fraser, commander, 30 men.
First Separate Company Rhode Island Militia,
Capt. R. W. Blunt, commander, 30 men.
Governor Ames, Hon. George F. Hoar, Mr. John Fiske, Mr. John Boyle O'Reilly, Rev. Andrew Chamberlain, Rev. Albert H. Plumb, D.D., Rev. Eli Smith, the Executive Council and heads of State Departments, members of Senate and House of Representatives, Mayor O'Brien and members of Board of Aldermen and Common Council, the Citizens' Committee, New York and Newport Fishing Club, represented by Commodore James W. Mars, Dr. P. W. Ray, and V. C. Murray, and other invited guests in carriages.

Allen's Fife and Drum Corps.
Robert A. Bell Post 134, G.A.R.,
Capt. I. S. Mullen, commander, 48 men.
Shaw Guard Veteran Association,
Major J. Wesley Furlong, commander, 40 men.
W. H. Carney Camp, S.V.,
Capt. John D. Powell, commander, 40 men,

UNVEILING THE MONUMENT. 33

with Captain Cushman, Lieutenant Clark,
and Captain Kelly, honorary staff.
Boston Brass Band, 30 men.
Boston Patriarchic No. 4, G.U.O. of O.F.,
H. Black, commander, 57 men.
Crispus Attucks Lodge K.P.,
George W. Winston, commander, 30 men.

Arriving at the monument, the procession entered the semi-diamond-shaped enclosure around it, and the State and city officials and the Citizens' Committee, with invited guests, occupied a platform erected in front of the monument; and in the midst of thousands of people, the ceremonies began a little past the noon hour.

The Germania Band played "America," and then the REV. ELI SMITH, of Springfield, offered the following prayer: —

PRAYER OFFERED BY REV. ELI SMITH.

O Lord, our Heavenly Father, we bow before Thee to-day in humble acknowledgment of Thy goodness and greatness. The heavens declare Thy glory, and the firmament showeth Thy handiwork. Before the mountains were brought forth, or ever Thou hadst formed this earth or the world, even from everlasting to everlasting, Thou art God. We rejoice that Thou hast ever borne rule in the affairs of men, and that Thou hast given nations to see Thy power and might. Thou wast Israel's God; and because they trusted in Thee, Thou didst work in a wonderful way with them, and didst cause them to become more powerful than all other nations besides. Thou wast their cloud by day, their pillar of fire by night; and Thou didst even make a way for them through the sea. It was only as they turned from following Thee, and became rebellious subjects, that they were discomfited before their enemies. As we look back over the history of the past, we are made to see that no nation or people have been destined to a very long or prosperous career that have not made the Lord their God. Help us, O Lord God, to take these things to heart; and as we desire success and perpetuity may we ever be loyal to Thee. Our thoughts now dwell upon two of the greatest struggles in which the American people have engaged, — the one of 1776, the other of 1861. We thank Thee that through the one the principle of no taxation without representation was vindicated, and that this country was severed from Great Britain; and that through the other the mistaken notions of the right of secession were settled by the sword, and human slavery forever abolished from our land. We thank Thee that in both these struggles there were engaged those of an oppressed race, who for centuries had been made to toil as bondmen. We thank Thee for the exhibitions they gave of patriotism, of love of country, when they themselves were without a country. We thank Thee that the first blood of the revolutionary conflict was shed by a black man, a representative of the race with whom so many of us here are identified. We take great pride in the fact that bravely he lost his life battling for the right. We rejoice that it is our privilege — a grand one may we esteem it — to do honor to-day to Crispus Attucks and his brave compatriots, in the very city where they fell, a century and more after the event. We thank Thee that Massachusetts, the Cradle of Liberty, — Massachusetts, foremost ever in that which is good; the birthplace of the anti-slavery movement; the home of Garrison, of Sumner, of Phillips, of Andrew, and of Wilson; the first to throw open her schools to the black man, and to recognize his manhood, — is also the first to do honor to him in rearing a monument to commemorate his valor and patriotism in a great conflict. May it be that Massachusetts shall feel, that as she by this monument is honoring the dead, and giving courage and hope to a race with whom one of the dead was identified, that so is she doing honor to herself. We pray Thee to bless the Governor of our Commonwealth and the Legislature of our State, also the Mayor of this city, to whom we are in so great measure indebted for the occasion given us to celebrate to-day. Help us to lay aside every weight and everything that may tend to retard our progress. Grant that all those plotting against the peace of our Government may be foiled in their schemes. Grant that the time may come, and hasten, we beseech Thee, its coming, when we shall know no North, no South, no East, or West; when race or creed shall not enter into the question of the solution of any of our problems of government; but when we shall be indeed *United States*, and the proudest boast of our citizens shall be that they are American citizens. Bless, we pray Thee, the President of these United States, and all associated with him in authority. Grant now to us O Lord, we do beseech Thee,

Thy Holy Spirit. Be Thou in the services of this day. May the words spoken by those who have been selected for the occasion not fall upon dull and inattentive hearers, but may they be as seed cast in good ground. Give it unto us in years to come, to look back with joy to this day as one of the brightest and best of our lives. And now we ask Thee to bless, comfort, sustain, and strengthen us; and to Thee, the only wise God, our Creator and Preserver, be praises, glory, and dominion, both now and forevermore. Amen.

Mr. WILLIAM H. DUPREE, chairman of the Citizens' Committee, then opened the formal exercises of the unveiling in the following words: —

Fellow-Citizens, — As chairman of the Committee of Arrangements, it becomes my duty to open the exercises that have been appointed for this time. In the occurrence which we commemorate, the colored race has a profound interest, for one of that race was the principal figure in it. From the sacrifice of that day, the people rose with new inspiration, — the determination to achieve their liberation, if not from foreign tyranny, at least from domestic oppression, was fixed by this. Whatever the immediate purpose was, it hastened the formal Declaration of Independence. On the fourth day of March, the British troops seemed to be immovably intrenched in Boston, and the enactments of their superiors were supposed to be the paramount law of the land. On the 5th, by the death of Attucks and his comrades, submission to English law gave place to active opposition; and when the governor would have compromised on the 6th by removing one of the two regiments from the town, the fervor and firmness of the people proved too much for him, and both regiments were taken away. The people were masters. The real authority had been wrested from the king, and assumed by his subjects. The death of these men made the republic secure. The events which followed were the necessary sequence of this, and so, on Sept. 3, 1788, the official stamp of legality and regularity was given to the "disorderly" attack on the troops thirteen years before.

It is well to raise monuments on the fields of Lexington and Bunker Hill, at Saratoga and Yorktown, to the defeats and triumphs of those times; but can any fact be more worthy of remembrance than the first and undisciplined resistance of those heroic souls that, aflame with the fire of freedom, would not wait to fight in well-formed battalions?

If there had been no commencement to the struggle, there would have been no end to it. Grand enterprises grow from small beginnings. Those who dare against the greatest odds deserve, in the event of ultimate success, the greatest praise. The importance of an action is measured by the final results of it. The republic started out in her career of enlarging freedom when the mercenaries of the crown were first forced from her soil.

The greatest thing about the late Civil War was

the abolition of slavery. The raid of John Brown commenced the effort; the emancipation proclamation concluded it. Brown led the march for freedom. The great thing about the war of the Revolution was the abolition of royal rule — the enthronement of popular sovereignty. Fate dictated the Peace of 1783, that for all peoples and for all times has forever affirmed the right of rebellion against tyranny when Attucks fell in 1770.

The Commonwealth of Massachusetts, recognizing the high importance of this date in our annals, has erected this monument in commemoration of it. It is the office of the chief representative of the State to unveil and present this memorial to you.

I have the honor to introduce His Excellency the Governor.

Governor AMES responded, as representing the Commonwealth, in the following words: —

Ladies and Gentlemen, — We meet here to-day to unveil a memorial of no common deed. We are about to show in all its significance a tribute to those who first gave their lives in that struggle with the mother country which led to our birth as a nation, and which gave us a chance to develop as a people. This is the first monument which the State has ever raised, although it has custody of many that have been presented to it; and in placing it where it is, the Commonwealth has sought, through its Governor and Council, to not only give it an appropriate situation, but to join with the city of Boston in its perpetual custody. The ready response of His Honor the Mayor to my suggestion that it be placed here, insures for it that care which we all desire.

I show to you all — and I bespeak for it careful inspection — the tribute in stone and bronze that Massachusetts erects to not the least of its heroes.

As the Governor closed, Miss Lillian E. Chappelle, daughter of Mr. J. C. Chappelle of the committee, pulled the string that bound the canopy of American tricolor that hid the monument, and it dropped gracefully to the pedestal, when there was a concerted shout of delight by the assembled thousands.

His Honor HUGH O'BRIEN, Mayor of Boston, was then introduced, and said: —

Mr. Chairman: Your Excellency, — On account of the exercises in Faneuil Hall I will merely say at this time that I accept this gift in the name of our citizens of Boston, and I congratulate you, Mr. Governor, that during your administration the State of Massachusetts has been patriotic enough to erect a monument to Crispus Attucks and his martyr associates.

The procession then re-formed and proceeded to Faneuil Hall, marching through Tremont, Court, and State streets to the site of the massacre, and thence down State to Merchants row to the Hall.

EXERCISES AT FANEUIL HALL.

EXERCISES AT FANEUIL HALL.

Faneuil Hall was crowded at the hour appointed for the exercises to commence by an audience composed of people from all parts of the Commonwealth and adjoining States.

On the platform, among others, were His Excellency Gov. Oliver Ames, Lieut.-Gov. J. Q. A. Brackett, Hon. George F. Hoar, ex-Gov. Alexander H. Rice, Hon. Henry B. Peirce, Mayor Hugh O'Brien, Hon. P. B. S. Pinchback, of Louisanna, Col. M. M. Cunniff, Curtis Guild, Jr., Charles Lincoln Smith, William W. Wheildon, T. A. Ridley, Joseph Lee, Lewis Hayden, Judge Cowley, of Lowell, Robert Treat Paine, Jr., Hon. John H. Smythe, ex-Minister to Liberia, Rev. A. A. Miner, D.D., Rev. J. C. Price, of Saulsbury, N.C., and the Citizens' Committee.

At 1.25 P.M. the Germania Band performed a medley of patriotic airs, at the conclusion of which the REV. ALBERT H. PLUMB, D.D., pastor of the Walnut Avenue Congregational Church, made the following prayer: —

Almighty God, the God of our fathers, we adore Thee as the Father of all flesh.

Thou hast "made of one blood all nations of men for to dwell on all the face of the earth," and Thy "tender mercies are over all Thy works."

In every age and every land and upon all peoples Thy bountiful benefactions have descended, and Thy providential guidance has been bestowed.

For, although we gratefully acknowledge that Thou hast shed peculiar blessings on this land and nation, as Thou didst on thy chosen people in ancient time, we adore the largeness of Thy purpose in our history as in theirs. Thou didst say to Abraham, the father of the faithful, the friend of God, "In thee shall all the families of the earth be blessed."

And "in the fulness of the time" of the seed of Abraham Thou didst send forth Thy Son, the Saviour of the world, "the one Mediator between God and men," "that He should taste death for every man."

And O Thou God of nations, who hast led forth the migrations of all wandering peoples, and hast hedged in the dwelling-places of the stable nations, we look with wonder and awe on the orderly procedure of Thy plans of mercy for all mankind in our own history, as Thou hast brought to these shores so many representatives of such various races of men. And we praise Thee that under the benign influence of the institutions Thou didst aid our fathers here to plant, there has been here enjoyed, in the sight of all nations and for the benefit of all, — more, we believe, than ever elsewhere before, — a practical recognition of those great truths, fundamental to all right social order, — the fatherhood of God, and the brotherhood of man.

O God, we confess with sorrow, that human history has been marred, and the upward progress of mankind delayed, by the practical denial of these truths. We mourn that in this guilt we ourselves have shared. Oh, help us sincerely to repent of all unfilial conduct towards Thee, of all unbrotherly feeling towards our brother-man.

Forgive us all our sins, through the mediation of Thy Son our Lord.

And may the commemorative exercises in which we are now engaged fill our hearts with new admiration for all heroic self-sacrifice for the honor of God and the good of man. Let Thy blessing rest on all who have aided in building the monument we dedicate this day. Smile, especially, we pray Thee, on Thy servants the Governor of this Commonwealth, and the chief magistrate of this city, that their official acts in these services may lead all the citizens whom they represent to cherish a larger reverence for liberty and law.

Open Thou our hearts to the words which shall be spoken by orator and poet, in praise of virtue and valor and resistance to wrong.

May the echo of the words here spoken, and the sight hereafter of the stones of memorial this day consecrated, — calling to mind the long-past hour when the soil of our streets was reddened by the blood of patriots of different lineage and color, — lead successive generations of men to cherish the spirit of charity and love towards all mankind.

Guard Thou our liberties, gracious God, our free ballot, our free press, our free schools.

And may liberty of thought, liberty of speech, and liberty of worship never perish from our land. And the glory shall be thine. Amen.

Chairman DUPREE then introduced His Excellency, Governor AMES, as the presiding officer of the occasion, and Governor AMES, coming forward amid applause, said: —

We have just come from our beloved Common, where has been unveiled a monument erected to the memory of a noble race and noble men. Those men who are our special guests to-day are representatives of a race whose brother, Attucks, was the first one to fall in that great massacre. The opinions of other and wiser men have been given, and I will only say that this is a most fitting tribute to the memory of an occasion which did much toward freeing our nation from British rule. Allow me to introduce your Mayor.

When the applause subsided, Mayor O'BRIEN said: —

Mr. Chairman, Ladies and Gentlemen, — I am aware that the monument to Crispus Attucks and his martyr associates has been the subject of more or less adverse criticism, and that by some they are looked upon as rioters, who deserved their fate. I look upon it from an entirely different standpoint. The Boston Massacre was one of the most important and exciting events that preceded our Revolution. The throwing of the tea overboard in Boston harbor, the Boston Massacre, Paul Revere's ride to Lexington, with other exciting events, had, no doubt, great influence in uniting the colonists as one man against unjust taxation and British oppression; made possible the war of the Revolution and the Declaration of Independence, that immortal document which pronounced all men free and equal without regard to color, creed, or nationality.

I rejoice with you, Mr. Chairman, that after the lapse of more than one hundred years, the erection of the Attucks Monument on Boston Common ratifies the words of that declaration, that all men are free and equal, without regard to color, creed, or nationality; and that the memory of the martyrs whose blood was shed in the cause of liberty in 1770 will thus be preserved and honored for all time.

The Germania Band again played patriotic music, and Governor Ames then introduced MR. JOHN FISKE, of Cambridge, the well-known historian and lecturer, who delivered the oration of the occasion amidst the closest attention of the great audience, who frequently interrupted the speaker with applause and various expressions of approval.

The REV. ANDREW CHAMBERLAIN, of New Bedford, was then introduced, and read with great satisfaction the poem written by MR. JOHN BOYLE O'REILLY.

At the conclusion of the poem, the REV. ALBERT H. PLUMB pronounced the benediction.

POEM

BY

JOHN BOYLE O'REILLY.

CRISPUS ATTUCKS.

NEGRO PATRIOT. — KILLED IN BOSTON, MARCH 5, 1770.

[The Boston Massacre, March 5, 1770, may be regarded as the first act in the drama of the American Revolution. "From that moment," said Daniel Webster, "we may date the severance of the British Empire." The presence of the British soldiers in King street excited the patriotic indignation of the people. . . . Led by Crispus Attucks, the mulatto slave, and shouting, "The way to get rid of these soldiers is to attack the main guard! strike at the root! this is the nest!" with more valor than discretion, they rushed to King street, and were fired upon by Captain Preston's company. Crispus Attucks was the first to fall: he and Samuel Gray and James Caldwell were killed on the spot. Samuel Maverick and Patrick Carr were mortally wounded. — *Historical Research, by George Livermore.* — *Mass. Hist. Society.*]

Where shall we seek for a hero, and where shall we find a story?
Our laurels are wreathed for conquest, our songs for completed glory;
But we honor a shrine unfinished, a column uncapped with pride,
If we sing the deed that was sown like seed when Crispus Attucks died.

Shall we take for a sign this Negro-slave, with unfamiliar name —
With his poor companions, nameless too, till their lives leaped forth in flame?
Yes, surely, the verdict is not for us to render or deny;
We can only interpret the symbol; God chose these men to die —
As teachers, perhaps, that to humble lives may chief award be made;
That from lowly ones and rejected stones the temple's base is laid!

When the bullets leaped from the British guns, no chance decreed their aim:
Men see what the royel hirelings saw — a multitude and a flame;
But beyond the flame a mystery; five dying men in the street,
While streams of severed races in the well of a nation meet!

Oh, blood of the people! changeless tide, through century, creed, and race!
Still one as the sweet salt sea is one, though tempered by sun and place;
The same in the ocean currents, and the same in the sheltered seas;
Forever the fountain of common hopes and kindly sympathies.
Indian and Negro, Saxon and Celt, Teuton and Latin and Gaul —
Mere surface shadow and sunshine, while the sounding unifies all!
One love, one hope, one duty theirs! No matter the time or ken,
There never was separate heart-beat in all the races of men!

But alien is one — of class, not race; he has drawn the line for himself;
His roots drink life from inhuman soil, from garbage of pomp and pelf;
He times his heart from the common beat, he has changed his life-stream's hue;
He deems his flesh to be finer flesh, he boasts that his blood is blue.
Patrician, aristocrat, tory, — whatever his age or name,
To the people's rights and liberties a traitor ever the same.
The natural crowd is a mob to him, their prayer a vulgar rhyme;
The freeman's speech is sedition, and the patriot's deed a crime.
Wherever the race, the law, the land, — whatever the time or throne,
The tory is always a traitor to every class but his own.

Thank God for a land where pride is clipped, where arrogance stalks apart;
Where law and song and loathing of wrong are words of the common heart;

Where the masses honor straightforward strength, and know when veins are bled
That the bluest blood is putrid blood — that the people's blood is red!

And honor to Crispus Attucks, who was leader and voice that day, —
The first to defy, and the first to die, with Maverick, Carr, and Gray.
Call it riot or revolution, his hand first clenched at the crown;
His feet were the first in perilous place to pull the king's flag down;
His breast was the first one rent apart that liberty's stream might flow;
For our freedom now and forever, his head was the first laid low.

Call it riot or revolution, or mob or crowd, as you may,
Such deaths have been seed of nations, such lives shall be honored for aye.
They were lawless hinds to the lackeys, but martyrs to Paul Revere;
And Otis and Hancock and Warren read spirit and meaning clear.
Ye teachers, answer! what shall be done when just men stand in the dock?
When the caitiff is robed in ermine, and his sworders keep the lock;
When torture is robbed of clemency, and guilt is without remorse;
When tiger and panther are gentler than the Christian slaver's curse;
When law is a satrap's menace, and order the drill of a horde —
Shall the people kneel to be trampled, and bare their neck to the sword?

Not so! by this Stone of Resistance that Boston raises here!
By the old North Church's lantern, and the watching of Paul Revere!

Not so! by Paris of 'Ninety-Three, and Ulster of 'Ninety-Eight!
By Toussaint in St. Domingo! by the horror of Delhi's gate!
By Adam's word to Hutchinson! by the tea that is brewing still!
By the farmers that met the soldiers at Concord and Bunker Hill!

Not so! not so! Till the world is done, the shadow of wrong is dread.
The crowd that bends to a lord to-day, to-morrow shall strike him dead.
There is only one thing changeless: the earth steals from under our feet,
The times and manners are passing moods, and the laws are incomplete;
There is only one thing changes not, one word that still survives —
The slave is the wretch who wields the lash, and not the man in gyves!

There is only one test of contract: is it willing, is it good?
There is only one guard of equal right, — the unity of blood.
There is never a mind unchained and true that class or race allows;
There is never a law to be obeyed that reason disavows;
There is never a legal sin but grows to the law's disaster.
The master shall drop the whip, and the slave shall enslave the master!

O Planter of seed in thought and deed! has the year of right revolved,
And brought the Negro patriot's cause with its problem to be solved?
His blood streamed first for the building, and through all the century's years,
Our growth of story and fame of glory are mixed with his blood and tears.
He lived with men like a soul condemned — derided, defamed, and mute;
Debased to the brutal level, and instructed to be a brute.

His virtue was shorn of benefit, his industry of reward;
His love! — O men, it were mercy to have cut affection's cord!
Through the night of his woe, no pity save that of his fellow-slave;
For the wage of his priceless labor, the scourging block and the grave!

And now, is the tree to blossom? Is the bowl of agony filled?
Shall the price be paid and the honor said and the word of outrage stilled?
And we who have toiled for freedom's law, have we sought for freedom's soul?
Have we learned at last that human right is not a part, but the whole?
That nothing is told while the clinging sin remains part unconfessed?
That the health of the nation is perilled if one man be oppressed?

Has he learned — the slave from the rice-swamps, whose children were sold — has he
With broken chains on his limbs, and the cry in his blood, "I am free?"
Has he learned through affliction's teaching what our Crispus Attucks knew —
When Right is stricken, the white and black are counted as one, not two?
Has he learned that his century of grief was worth a thousand years
In blending his life and blood with ours, and that all his toils and tears
Were heaped and poured on him suddenly, to give him a right to stand
From the gloom of African forests in the blaze of the freest land?
That his hundred years have earned for him a place in the human van
Which others have fought for and thought for since the world of wrong began?

For this shall his vengeance change to love, and his retribution burn,
Defending the right, the weak and the poor, when each shall have his turn.
For this shall he set his woful past afloat on the stream of night;
For this he forgets, as we all forget, when darkness turns to light;
For this he forgives, as we all forgive, when wrong has changed to right.

And so must we come to the learning of Boston's lesson to-day;
The moral that Crispus Attucks taught in the old heroic way, —
God made mankind to be one in blood, as one in spirit and thought;
And so great a boon, by a brave man's death, is never dearly bought!

ADDRESS

BY

MR. JOHN FISKE.

THE "BOSTON MASSACRE."

We have met here to-day, in the venerable building which has so long been known to Americans as the Cradle of Liberty, to commemorate one of the most significant and impressive events in the noble struggle in which our forefathers succeeded in vindicating, for themselves and their posterity, the sacred right of self-government. Among the incidents of that stirring period, there are perhaps none more worthy of our careful study than those which attended the compulsory withdrawal from Boston of the troops which had been sent here for the purpose of intimidating its citizens and aiding in the enforcement of an odious system of revenue laws which the people had had no voice in making, and to which it was impossible for them tamely to submit without losing their own self-respect and imperilling the safety and happiness of future generations. When John Adams, in alluding long afterward to the memorable 5th of March, 1770, declared that "on that night the foundation of American independence was laid," he spoke with the vehement emphasis that was customary with him. Yet while it may not be necessary to adopt the statement in all its literal force, it serves to show us how deeply the events of that evening were graven upon the writer's mind; and it recalls with such vividness the temper and spirit of the time, as to lead us back to the true historical point of view. There is a sense in which John Adams' remark was quite true. In order to point out the real significance of the Boston Massacre and its place in American history, I must invite your attention for a few moments to the circumstances which led to the presence of British troops in Boston from the autumn of 1768 to the spring of 1770.

The troubles and disorders in Boston which led to the Revolution began soon after the grant of writs of assistance to the revenue officers in 1761. These writs of assistance were general search-warrants, empowering the collectors of customs to enter houses or shops in search of smuggled goods, but without specifying either houses or goods. This made it possible for a revenue officer to visit anybody's house, — perhaps from mere private spite, — and lay hands upon such articles as it might please him to condemn as having been brought into town without paying duty. The exercise of such an odious tyranny was sure to be resisted, and it was resisted. During the next half-dozen years, there were many instances in which warehouse doors were barricaded and the officers successfully defied. Into the midst of this irritation came the Stamp Act of 1765, a law which was repealed the next year because it was found impossible to enforce it in any of the colonies. The immediate fruits of the Stamp Act were riots in New York and Boston and elsewhere; and one of these riots in Boston was perhaps the most shameful affair in all the history of this town. It is quite characteristic of mob law to strike in the wrong places, and to punish those who have not offended. An impression got abroad that Chief Justice Hutchinson had favored the passage of the Stamp Act, and had acted as an informer against certain merchants suspected of breaking the revenue laws. This impression was entirely incorrect, but under the influence of it, one night in August, 1765, a drunken mob broke into Mr. Hutchinson's house, threw his furniture and pictures into the street, and destroyed the noble library which he had been thirty years in collecting, and which contained many priceless historical documents, the loss of which can never be repaired. Let us here particularly observe that this disgraceful affair was at once disowned and condemned by the people of Boston. Before Governor Bernard next morning had time to summon the Council, a town-meeting here in Faneuil Hall had expressed its abhorrence of the work of the rioters, and similar expressions of feeling were soon heard from town-meetings all over the Commonwealth. The ring-leaders were imprisoned, and the Legislature, chosen by the people, hastened to indemnify Mr. Hutchinson, so far as possible, for the damage inflicted by the mob. This incident shows conclusively that the people of Massachusetts felt no sympathy for rioters; and it should be borne in mind when we come to consider the very different feelings which were called forth by the circumstances of the Boston Massacre. Let us not fail to note that the great popular leader, Samuel Adams, whom the loyalists were fond of calling the "chief incendiary," was emphatic in his condemnation of the Hutchinson riot. One of Adams' favorite maxims was, "Always keep your enemy in the wrong." He knew that the American people were in the right, and therefore always appealed to reason, and always deprecated any resort to violence.

We may now pass to the year 1767, when Parliament, under the lead of Charles Townshend, passed a new revenue law for America. If the old revenue laws were odious because of the harsh way in which they were enforced, this act of 1767 was doubly odious because of the principle which it involved. Hitherto such acts had been passed with the design of regulating the commerce of the British Empire. This Townshend act, in laying duties upon tea and other articles, had a very different purpose. Under pretence of regulating commerce, it sought to deprive the Americans of their right of self-government. This was at once evident from the way in which the revenue derived from the tea and other articles was to be used. It was to be used for defraying the cost of a civil service to be established in all the colonies, and to be directly responsible to the crown. There had been much dispute for fifty years as to the way in which the governors' salaries should be paid. The act of 1767 was the prelude to a series of measures for taking this question out of the hands of the people entirely. It was five years more before the most serious of these measures, attacking the independence of the judges, was passed; but the whole policy of the British Government was so clearly indicated in the preamble to the act of 1767 that the Americans could not mistake it. People often talk as if the American Revolution originated in a mere money dispute, or else in some theoretical discussion over the right of representation. This is a grave mistake. It was far from being a mere question of paying duties, and there was much more in it than an assertion of abstract principle. It was something that came home with grim reality to everybody's door. Tea was selected as the chief article for taxation, because it was supposed that people could not get along without it. In its act of 1767, the British Government said to the American people, " We know very well that your wives and daughters will never give up their quiet social entertainments, in which tea is deemed indispensable. We are therefore going to tax that article, and with the money which you thus cannot help paying, we are going to defray the salaries of your governors and judges, and thus make them entirely independent of you, and responsible only to us." What was this but a shameless demand that the American people should part with their liberty? It was answered in three ways. Merchants in all the colonies answered by forming associations pledged to buy no more goods of any sort from England until the act of 1767 should be repealed. The ladies answered by forming associations pledged to wear homespun clothes and drink no more tea until the Government should retreat from its position. The Massachusetts Assembly answered in 1768 by its famous circular letter addressed to the other colonies, inviting them to coöperate with Massachusetts in resisting the enforcement of the law, and in petitioning for its prompt repeal.

This circular letter enraged King George and his ministers, and an order in council presently called upon the Massachusetts Assembly to rescind it. At the same time orders were sent to the assemblies of all the other colonies, forbidding them to pay any heed to the Massachusetts circular, under penalty of instant dissolution. Thus said the king, and how was he answered? For the first time, perhaps, in any American legislative body, there was uttered a threat of rebellion. "We are asked to rescind, are we?" said James Otis; "let Great Britain rescind her measures, or the colonies are lost to her forever!" After a debate of nine days, the Massachusetts Assembly decided, by a vote of ninety-two to seventeen, that it would *not* rescind its circular letter. The Assembly was immediately dissolved by Governor Bernard, but its vote was hailed with delight all over the country, and "the Illustrious Ninety-two" became the favorite toast on all convivial occasions. In several other colonies the assemblies passed resolutions expressing their sympathy with Massachusetts, and for so doing they were turned out of doors by the governors, in conformity to the royal order.

A decisive issue was thus rapidly forming between

the colonies and the crown; and as the freedom of
all was alike involved in it, the way was fast being
smoothed for the beginnings of the American Union.
As the ministry were inclined to try conclusions,
especially with Massachusetts and with Boston, everything that was done here for the next seven years
was watched with intense interest, and was fraught
with peculiar significance for the whole country. In
the spring of 1768, the fifty-gun frigate "Romney"
was sent to mount guard in Boston harbor and aid
the revenue commissioners; and while she lay there,
several of the citizens were seized and impressed as
seamen.

Now, while the town was very indignant over
this lawless kidnapping of its citizens, on the 10th
of June, John Hancock's sloop "Liberty" was
seized at the wharf by a boat's crew from the
"Romney," for an alleged violation of the revenue
laws, though without official warrant. Insults and
recriminations ensued between the officers and the
citizens assembled on the wharf, until after a
while the excitement grew into a mild form of
riot, in which a few windows were broken, some
of the officers were pelted, and finally a pleasure-
boat belonging to the collector was pulled up out
of the water, carried to the Common, and burned
there, — when, at length, Hancock and Adams arriving upon the scene, put a stop to the commotion.
A few days afterward a town-meeting was held in
Faneuil Hall; but as the crowd was too great to be
contained in the building, it was adjourned to the

Old South Meeting-House, where Otis addressed the people from the pulpit. A petition to the Governor was prepared, in which it was set forth that the impressment of peaceful citizens was an illegal act, and that the state of the town was as if war had been declared against it; and the Governor was requested to order the instant removal of the frigate from the harbor. A committee of twenty-one leading citizens was appointed to deliver this petition to the Governor at his house in Jamaica Plain. In his letters to the Secretary of State, Bernard professed to live in constant fear of assassination, and was always begging for troops to protect him against the incendiary and blackguard mob of Boston. Yet, as he looked down the beautiful road from his open window that summer afternoon, what he saw was not a ragged mob armed with knives and bludgeons, shouting "Liberty or death," and bearing the head of a revenue collector aloft on the point of a pike,— what he saw was a quiet procession of eleven chaises, from which there alighted at his door twenty-one gentlemen, as sedate and stately in demeanor as those old Roman senators at whom the Gaulish chief so marvelled. There followed a very affable interview, during which wine was passed around; and next day the Governor's answer was read in town-meeting, declining to remove the frigate, but promising that in future there should be no more impressment of Massachusetts citizens; and with this compromise the wrath of the people was, for the moment, assuaged.

Affairs of this sort, reported with gross exaggeration by the Governor and revenue commissioners to the ministry, produced in England the impression that Boston was a lawless and riotous town, full of cutthroats and blacklegs, whose violence could only be held in check by martial law. Of all the misconceptions of America by England which brought about the American Revolution, perhaps this notion of the extreme turbulence of Boston was the most ludicrous. During the ten years of excitement which preceded the war of independence, if we except the one shameful riot in which Hutchinson's house was sacked, there was much less uproar and confusion in Boston than might reasonably have been expected. In all this time not a drop of blood was shed by the people, nor was anybody's life for a moment in danger at their hands. The only fit ground for wonder is that they behaved themselves so quietly. The disturbance attending the seizure of the sloop "Liberty" was a fair sample of the disorders which occurred at moments of extreme excitement, and it was nothing compared to the riots which used to happen in London in those days. "The worst you could say about Boston," observed Colonel Barré in Parliament, "was that she was imitating the mother-country."

Even before the affair of the "Liberty," the Government had made up its mind to send troops to Boston. The avowed purpose in sending them was to preserve order; and such events as the sacking of Hutchinson's house must have gone far toward creating in England a public opinion which should sanction such a measure. But beneath this avowed purpose lay the ultimate purpose, on the part of the king and his friends, of intimidating the popular party and enforcing the Townshend act. The people of Boston understood this perfectly well. They knew that the Townshend act was contrary to the whole spirit of the British constitution; and in this they were at one with many of the ablest and most liberal statesmen of England. There were no disorders that had not directly originated in British aggression, — not one. Let this unjust and mischievous act of legislation be repealed, and there would be no disorders to be repressed. Whatever the ostensible purpose by which the sending of these troops was justified to the British people, there could be no doubt as to its real meaning. It meant the substitution of brute force for argument; it meant military tyranny. And this, I say, the people of Boston knew full well, although some of their descendants seem to have forgotten it.

In September, 1768, it was announced in Boston that the troops were on their way, and would soon be landed. There happened to be a legal obstacle, unforeseen by the ministry, to their being quartered in the city. In accordance with the general act of Parliament for quartering troops, the regular barracks at Castle William in the harbor would have to be filled before the town could be required to find quarters for any troops. Another clause of the act provided that if any military officer should take upon himself to quarter soldiers in any of His

Majesty's dominions, otherwise than as allowed by the act, he should straightway be dismissed the service. At the news that the troops were about to arrive, the Governor was asked to convene the Assembly, that it might be decided how to receive them. On Bernard's refusal, the selectmen of Boston issued a circular, inviting all the towns of Massachusetts to send delegates to a general convention, in order that deliberate action might be taken upon this important matter. In answer to the circular, delegates from ninety-six towns assembled in Faneuil Hall, and, laughing at the Governor's order to "disperse," proceeded to show how, in the exercise of the undoubted right of public meeting, the colony could virtually legislate for itself in the absence of its regular Legislature. The convention, finding that nothing was necessary for Boston to do but insist upon strict compliance with the letter of the law, adjourned. In October, two regiments — the Fourteenth and Twenty-ninth — arrived, and were allowed to land without opposition, but no lodging was provided for them. Governor Bernard, in fear of an affray, had gone out into the country; but nothing could have been further from the thoughts of the people. The commander, Colonel Dalrymple of the Fourteenth, requested shelter for his men, but was told that he must quarter them in the barracks at Castle William. As the night was frosty, however, they were compassionately allowed to sleep in Faneuil Hall. Next day the Governor, finding everything quiet, came back, and heard Dalrymple's complaint. But in vain did he apply in turn to the Council, to the selectmen, and to the justices of the peace, to grant quarters for the troops: he was told that the law was plain, and that the Castle must first be occupied. The Governor then tried to get possession of an old dilapidated building which belonged to the colony, but the tenants had taken legal advice, and told him to turn them out if he dared. Nothing could be more provoking. General Gage was obliged to come on from his headquarters at New York; but not even he, the commander-in-chief of His Majesty's forces in America, could quarter the troops in violation of the statute, without running the risk of being cashiered on conviction before two justices of the peace. So the soldiers stayed in tents on the Common, until the weather grew so cold that Dalrymple was obliged to hire some buildings for them at exorbitant rates and at the expense of the crown. By the time this question was settled, two more regiments — the Sixty-fourth and Sixty-fifth — had arrived, and were quartered in some large storehouses on Wheelwright's wharf. The Fourteenth was quartered in a building on Brattle street, owned by James Murray, and henceforth known as "Murray's Barracks;" the Twenty-ninth was quartered between King and Water streets; and the main guard was accommodated in King street near the Town House. Small detachments were posted at the ferries and on Boston Neck, and two cannon were planted on King street with their muzzles pointing toward the

Town House — for what purpose it would be hard to say; but it could hardly be otherwise interpreted by the people than as a menace and an insult.

No sooner were the soldiers thus established in Boston than Samuel Adams published the series of letters signed "Vindex," in which he argued that to quarter an army among the people of Massachusetts without the consent of the Legislature was as unjustifiable and as gross a violation of the Bill of Rights as it would be to quarter an army in London without the consent of Parliament. In other words, the troops were intruders and trespassers in Boston; they had no right to be here at all, since the Government had transcended its constitutional powers in sending them. This was part and parcel of Adams' doctrine, that the Massachusetts Legislature was as supreme in Massachusetts as the Parliament in Great Britain; that Americans must be governed by lawmakers chosen by themselves, and not by law-makers chosen by other people. It was to maintain this doctrine that the Revolutionary War was fought; and our forefathers, who maintained it, were quite right in holding that the soldiers were intruders, who might with entire propriety be warned off the premises or forcibly ejected, should occasion require it. For the present the milder course of petition to the king was the proper one; and in the annual March meeting of 1769, a paper was adopted, praying for the removal of the troops. In April the ministry, without consulting Governor Bernard, instructed General Gage at New York to use his own discretion as to keeping the troops at Boston or withdrawing them. Early in June Gage ordered the Sixty-fourth and Sixty-fifth Regiments away from Boston, and in the letter in which he advised Bernard of this order, he asked him if it would not be better to remove the other two regiments also. The citizens, hearing of this, held a town-meeting, and declared that the civil magistrates were quite able to protect life and property, so that the mere presence of the troops was an insult to the town. Bernard, however, wrote to Gage that it would not be prudent to remove the troops, though perhaps one regiment in the town and one at the Castle might be enough. The result was that nothing more was done, and the Fourteenth and Twenty-ninth Regiments remained at their quarters. In July, Bernard sailed for England, leaving affairs in the hands of Hutchinson as lieutenant-governor.

While these things were going on, the soldiers did many things that greatly annoyed the people. They led brawling, riotous lives, and made the quiet streets hideous by night with their drunken shouts. Scores of loose women, who had followed the regiments across the ocean, came to scandalize the town for a while, and then to encumber the almshouse. On Sundays the soldiers would race horses on the Common, or would play "Yankee Doodle" just outside the church-doors during the services. Now and then oaths, or fisticuffs, or blows with sticks were exchanged between soldiers and citizens, and at length a much more serious affair occurred. One evening in September a dastardly assault was made upon James Otis at the British Coffee House by one Robinson, a Commissioner of Customs, assisted by half a dozen army officers. It was a strange parallel to the assault upon Charles Sumner by Brooks of South Carolina, shortly before the War of Secession. Otis was savagely beaten, and received a blow on the head with a sword, from the effects of which he never recovered, but finally lost his reason. The popular wrath at this outrage was intense, but there was no disturbance. Otis brought suit against Robinson, and recovered two thousand pounds in damages, but refused to accept a penny of it when Robinson confessed himself in the wrong, and humbly asked pardon for his irreparable offence.

During the next six months the tension of feeling steadily increased. Dr. Franklin wrote from London that he lived in constant dread of the news of some outbreak that might occasion irreparable mischief. In the course of February, 1770, there was an unusual number of personal encounters. In one or two instances criminals were forcibly rescued from the hands of the constable. Citizens were pricked with bayonets. On the 22d of that month, a well-known informer named Richardson, being pelted by a party of school-boys, withdrew into his house, opened a window, and fired at random into the crowd, killing a little boy, Christopher Snyder, about eleven years of age, and severely wounding a son of Capt. John Gore. The funeral of the murdered boy took place on Monday, the 26th, and was attended by a grand procession of citizens. It was with some difficulty that Richardson, on his way to jail, was protected from the wrath of the people. On his trial in April he was convicted of murder, but after two years in prison was pardoned. We can well understand that the state of feeling in the days following the little boy's funeral must have been extremely intense. Quarrels and blows were constantly occurring that week. The Twenty-ninth Regiment, according to Hutchinson, contained a number of rough and ill-disciplined fellows, and as their quarters were very near Mr. John Gray's ropewalk, they came into frequent collision with the workmen.

On Friday things assumed a decidedly warlike aspect. About noon a soldier put his head into one of the windows of the ropewalk, and gave vent to his spleen in oaths and taunts, until presently a workman came out and knocked him down, while another took away his sword. The soldier then went to the barracks and returned with a dozen companions armed with clubs. A fight ensued, in which the soldiers were worsted, and beat a retreat. Presently they returned again, reenforced to the number of thirty or forty; but all hands in the ropewalk were now ready to receive them, and they were again beaten off with bruises and scars. Cutlasses were used, and some blood was drawn, though no one was seriously hurt. On Saturday, Colonel Carr, commander of the Twenty-ninth, complained to Governor Hutchinson; and on Monday the complaint was laid before the Council, and several members of that body declared their opinion that the only way of insuring against a deadly affray was to withdraw the two regiments from the town to the Castle. In the afternoon a hand-bill was posted by the soldiers, informing the rebellious people of Boston that they were determined to join together and defend themselves against all opponents. There was some anxiety among the citizens, and people gathered in groups on street-corners, discussing the situation. The loud and angry threats of the soldiers led many to believe that a massacre was intended. It was time, they said, to wet their bayonets in the blood of these New England people. At about eight in the evening, a crowd collected near the barracks in Brattle street. Conspicuous among the throng was a very tall colored man, who seemed to be acting as a leader. From bandying abusive epithets with the soldiers, the crowd went on to pelt them with snowballs, while, in turn, blows were dealt with the butt-ends of muskets. Presently, Captain Goldfinch coming along, ordered his men into their barracks for the night, and thus seemed to have stopped the affray. But meanwhile some one had got into the Old Brick Meeting-house, opposite the head of King street, — where the Sears Building now stands — and rung the bell; and this, being interpreted as an alarm of fire, brought out many more people into the moonlit streets. It was now a little past nine o'clock. Bands of soldiers and of citizens were hurrying hither and thither, and the accounts of what happened are as disorderly and conflicting as the incidents which they try to relate. There were cries of "Town-born, turn out! the redcoats are going to kill us!" and responses from the soldiers, "Damn you, we will walk a lane through you all!" Between the limits of what are now known as Dock square and School street in the one direction, and Scollay square and Long wharf in the other, there was the surging of the crowd, — not a vast and continuous crowd, but a series of groups of enraged men, gesticulating and cursing, actuated by no definite plan, but simply giving incoherent utterance to the passions which had been so long restrained, and were at last wrought up beyond endurance.

In Dock square, "a tall gentleman in a large white wig and red cloak" harangued the crowd for a few minutes, and they listened quietly while he was speaking. Who this mysterious person was, or what he said, has never been ascertained. Presently there was a shout of "Hurrah for the main guard! there is the nest!" and the crowd began pouring into King street, through Exchange lane, while the tall colored man, whose name was Crispus Attucks, led a party in the same direction through the lower part of Cornhill, now included in Washington street.

In front of the Custom House, on the corner of King street and Exchange lane, a sentinel was pacing. A few minutes before, as Captain Goldfinch passed by on his way to stop the affray in Brattle street, a barber's apprentice had reviled him for having had his hair dressed and gone off without paying. The sentinel knocked the boy down, and was forthwith pelted with snowballs by other boys. While this was going on, the crowd from Dock square arrived upon the scene, and the sentinel retreated up the steps of the Custom House, and called for help. Some one ran to the guard-house and cried, "They are killing the sentinel; turn out the guard!" Captain Preston and seven or eight privates from the Twenty-ninth came up the street upon the double-quick, prodding people with their bayonets and shouting, "Make way, damn you, make way!"—"Are you going to murder people?" asked a sailor. "Yes, by God! root and branch," was the reply. As the soldiers formed in a half-circle around the sentry-box, and Preston ordered them to prime and load, the bookseller Henry Knox, afterward major-general in the Continental Army, seized the captain by the coat, and warned him that if blood was shed he would have to answer for it with his life. "I know it," said Preston. "I hope," said another gentleman, "you do not intend to fire on the people."—"By no means," said Preston. The crowd pressed up to the muzzles of the guns, threw snow in the soldiers' faces, and dared them to fire. Amid the clamor and scurry there were so many cries of "Fire!" that it would not have been strange had some one of them been mistaken for an order. It is most likely that no such order was given by Preston; but all at once seven of the levelled pieces were discharged, not simultaneously, but in quick succession like the striking of a clock. The first shot, fired by a soldier named Montgomery, killed Crispus Attucks, who was standing quietly at a little distance leaning upon a stick. The second, fired by one Kilroy, slew Samuel Gray, who was just stepping toward the fallen Attucks. The next killed James Caldwell, a sailor, standing in the middle of the street. Samuel Maverick, a boy of seventeen, and Patrick Carr had heard the church-bell, and come out to see where the fire was. They were shot and mortally wounded as they were crossing the street. Maverick died next morning, Carr nine days later. Six other men fell, dangerously, but not fatally, wounded.

The church-bells now began pealing, the alarm was spread through the town, people flocked by hundreds to the scene, the drums beat to arms, the Twenty-ninth Regiment was called out and drawn up for platoon-firing, and a general slaughter seemed imminent, when the arrival of Hutchinson put an end to the tumult. The scholarly lieutenant-governor, in his study in North square, had heard the bells, and supposed there was a fire somewhere; but soon there came knocks at his front door, and flurried and breathless cries that "the troops had risen on the people." Making all haste to King street, he shouted indignantly to Preston, "Are you the commanding officer?" — "Yes, sir." — "What do you mean by firing on the people without an order from a civil magistrate." All that could be heard of Preston's reply was something about saving the sentry. A sudden surge of the crowd pushed Hutchinson in through the door of the Town House. He ran up-stairs into the Council Chamber and came out on the balcony. In spite of his Tory sympathies, his lofty character and the memory of his splendid public services still gave him much weight with the people, and they listened quietly as he addressed them. A court of inquiry was ordered, the soldiers were sent to their barracks, Preston and his squad were arrested, the people slowly dispersed to their homes, and it was three o'clock in the morning before Hutchinson left the scene.

In the forenoon the Council advised the removal of the offending regiment, — the Twenty-ninth, — but in the afternoon an immense town-meeting, called at Faneuil Hall, adjourned to the Old South Meeting-house; and as they passed by the Town House, the lieutenant-governor, looking out upon their march, judged "their spirit to be as high as was the spirit of their ancestors when they imprisoned Andros, while they were four times as numerous." All the way from the church to the Town House the street was crowded with the people, while a committee, headed by Samuel Adams, waited upon the lieutenant-governor, and received his assurance that the Twenty-ninth Regiment should be removed. As the committee came out from the Town House to carry the lieutenant-governor's reply to the meeting in the church, the people pressed back on either side to let them pass; and Adams, leading the way with uncovered head through the lane thus formed, and bowing first to one side and then to the other, passed along the watchword "Both regiments or none!" When, in the church, the question was put to vote, three thousand voices shouted, "Both regiments or none!" and armed with this ultimatum the committee returned to the Town House, where the lieutenant-governor was seated with Colonel Dalrymple and the members of the Council. Then Adams, in quiet but earnest tones, stretching forth his arm and pointing his finger at Hutchinson, reminded him that if, as royal governor of the province, he had the power to remove one regiment, he had equally the power to remove both; that the voice of three thousand freemen demanded that all soldiery be forthwith removed from the town; and that if he failed to heed their just demands, he did so at his peril. "I observed his knees to tremble," said the old hero afterward, "I saw his face grow pale, and I enjoyed the sight!" Before sundown the order had gone forth for the removal of both regiments to Castle William, and not until then did the meeting in the church break up.

It has often been remarked that this scene in the Council Chamber would make a fine subject for an historical painting. This removal of the instruments of tyranny at the behest of a New England town-meeting was certainly one of the most impressive scenes in history, and it summed up the coming Revolution as an overture sums up the musical drama to which it is prefixed. It was four years before British troops were again quartered in Boston; and on the sixth anniversary of the memorable scene in the Council Chamber, General Howe looked with rueful gaze at Washington's threatening batteries on Dorchester Heights, and decided that it was high time to retreat from the town. When the news of the affray in King street, and the consequent removal of the troops, reached England, the king's friends were chagrined, and there was some discussion in Parliament as to whether it would do to submit tamely to such a defeat. It was suggested that the troops ought to be ordered back into the town, when Colonel Barré pithily asked, "If, under the circumstances, the commanders over there saw fit to remove the troops, what minister here will venture to order them back?" As nobody was ready with a reply to this question, the subject was dropped; but for many years afterwards the Fourteenth and Twenty-ninth Regiments were familiarly known in Parliament as "The Sam Adams Regiments."

It was the sacrifice of the lives of Crispus Attucks, Samuel Gray, James Caldwell, Samuel Maverick, and Patrick Carr that brought about this preliminary victory of the American Revolution. Their death effected in a moment what seventeen months of petition and discussion had failed to accomplish. Instead of the king's representatives intimidating the people of Boston, it was the people of Boston that had intimidated the king's representatives. Nature is apt to demand some forfeit in accomplishing great results, and for achieving this particular result the lives of those five men were the forfeit. It is, therefore, historically correct to regard them as the first martyrs to the cause of American independence; as such they have long deserved a monument in the most honorable place that Boston could give for the purpose, and such a place is Boston Common. If experience did not teach us how full the world is of paradox and looseness of thought, I should deem it incredible that any student of history should ever have doubted so plain and obvious a conclusion. The present generation of historical students is very creditably engaged in attempts to do justice to the motives of the Tories of the Revolution, who have, in many instances, been maligned and misunderstood. Such attempts deserve our warmest sympathy, for it is the duty of the historian to understand the past, and only in so far as he divests himself of partisan prejudice can he understand it. But in order to be fair toward Tories, it is not necessary to become Tories ourselves. We seem to be in some danger of forgetting this obvious caution. Some of our scholars seem to have swung around into the Tory view of the events which ushered in the Revolution, and things have been said about the Boston Massacre which one would think fit to make glorious old Samuel Adams turn in his grave. The motives and purposes of the victims have been belittled or aspersed. In truth, we know little or nothing about their motives and purposes; but we may fairly suppose them to have been actuated by the same feelings toward the soldiery that animated Adams and Warren and the patriots of Boston in general. The five victims were obscure men. As we have lately been reminded, they did not belong to our "first families." This, however, did not prevent Doctor Warren from calling them "our slaughtered brethren," and I do not suppose anybody that heard this phrase from the lips of that high-minded patriot would have attributed it to a seeking after political effect. The immense concourse of people, including our "first families," that followed them on the 8th of March to their grave in the Old Granary Burying-ground, unquestionably regarded them as victims who had suffered in the common cause. Of their personal history next to nothing is known. Three of them — Caldwell, Carr, and Maverick — would seem to have been by-standers accidentally shot. Of the two who took a prominent part in the affair, Gray was one of the workmen at the ropewalk; Attucks was a stranger in Boston. He was a sailor employed on Captain Folger's whaleship from Nantucket, which was lying in Boston harbor. He was described as a mulatto, and may very probably have been the slave Crispus, six feet two inches in height, who ran away from his master, William Browne, of Framingham, in the fall of 1750, and was duly advertised in the "Boston Gazette" of November 20, in that year. If that be the case, he was about forty-six years old at the time of his death. It has also been argued that he may have been a Natick Indian, since the name Attucks is certainly an Indian name signifying "deer." Quite likely he had both Indian and African blood in his veins; such a thing was not unusual in the country about Framingham. At the time of his death his home is said to have been in the Island of Nassau, and he was apparently embarked for North Carolina, working his way, perhaps, towards his home. From this time until independence was won, there was hardly a struggle in which brave men of his race and color did not nobly acquit themselves.

Such was the famous "Boston Massacre." The excellent British historian, Mr. Lecky, observes that "there are many dreadful massacres recorded in the pages of history, — the massacre of the Danes by the Saxons, the Massacre of the Sicilian Vespers, the Massacre of St. Bartholomew, — but it may be questioned whether any of them produced such torrents of indignant eloquence as this affair." (Hist. Eng. III., 367.) In commenting upon the very gentle sarcasm here implied, I would remind Mr. Lecky that it will not do to try to measure history with a foot-rule. Lord Sherbrooke — better known as Robert Lowe — declared a few years ago, in a speech on the uses of a classical education, that the Battle of Marathon was really of less account than a modern colliery-explosion, because only one hundred and ninety-two of the Greek army lost their lives. From such a point of view, one might argue that the "Boston Massacre" was an event of far less importance than an ordinary free fight among Colorado gamblers. It is needless to say that this is not the historical point of view. Historically, the "Boston Massacre" is not only important from the fresh impetus it gave to the nascent revolutionary feeling among the Americans at that time, but it furnishes an instructive illustration of the high state of civilization that had been attained by the people among whom it happened, — by the oppressors as well as those whom it was sought to oppress. The quar-

tering of troops in a peaceful town is something
that has in most ages been regarded with horror.
Under the senatorial government of Rome, it used
to be said that the quartering of troops, even upon
a friendly province and for the purpose of protecting
it, was a visitation only less to be dreaded than an
inroad of hostile barbarians. When we reflect that
the British regiments were encamped in Boston during seventeen months, among a population to whom
they were thoroughly odious, the fact that only half
a dozen persons lost their lives, and that otherwise
no really grave crimes seem to have been committed,
is a fact highly creditable both to the discipline of
the soldiers and to the moderation of the people.
In most ages and countries the shooting of half a
dozen citizens under such circumstances would either
have produced but a slight impression, or, on the
other hand, would perhaps have resulted on the spot
in a wholesale slaughter of the offending soldiers.
The fact that so profound an impression was made
in Boston and throughout the country, while at the
same time the guilty parties were left to be dealt
with in the ordinary course of law, is a striking
commentary upon the general peacefulness and de-
corum of American life; and it shows how high and
severe was the standard by which our forefathers
judged all lawless proceedings. And here it may
not be irrelevant to add that, throughout the constitutional struggles which led to the Revolution, the
American standard of political right and wrong was
so high that contemporary European politicians found

it sometimes difficult to understand it. And for a
like reason, even the most fair-minded modern
English historians sometimes fail to see why the
Americans should have been so quick to take offence
at acts of the British Government which doubtless
were not meant to be oppressive. If George III.
had been a bloodthirsty despot, like Philip II., of
Spain; if General Gage had been like the Duke of
Alva; if American citizens by the hundred had been
burned alive or broken on the wheel in New York
and Boston; if towns such as Providence and Hartford
had been given up to the cruelty and lust of
a beastly soldiery,—then no one would ever have
found it hard to understand why the Americans
should have exhibited a rebellious temper. But it is
one signal characteristic of the progress of political
civilization, that the part played by sheer brute force
in a barbarous age is fully equalled by the part
played by a mere covert threat of injustice in a
more advanced age. The effect which a blow in the
face would produce upon a barbarian will be wrought
upon a civilized man by an assertion of some far-
reaching legal principle, which only in a subtle and
ultimate analysis includes the possibility of a blow
in the face. From this point of view, the quickness
with which such acts as those of Charles Townshend
were comprehended in their remotest bearings is the
most striking proof one could wish of the high
grade of political culture which our forefathers had
reached through their system of perpetual free
discussion in town-meeting. They had, moreover,

reached a point where any manifestation of simple brute force in the course of a political dispute was exceedingly disgusting and shocking to them. To their minds the careless or wanton slaughter of five citizens conveyed just as much meaning as a St. Bartholomew massacre would have conveyed to the minds of men in a lower stage of political development.

It was not strange, therefore, that Samuel Adams and his friends should have been ready to make the "Boston Massacre" the occasion of a moral lesson to their contemporaries. As far as the offending soldiers were concerned, they were most honorably dealt with. There was no attempt to wreak a paltry vengeance on them. Brought to trial on a charge of murder, after a judicious delay of seven months, they were ably defended by John Adams and Josiah Quincy, and all were acquitted save Montgomery and Kilroy, who were convicted of manslaughter, and branded in the hand. There were some hot-heads who grumbled at the verdict, but the people of Boston generally acquiesced in it, as they showed by choosing John Adams for their representative in the Assembly. At the same time, such an event as the "Boston Massacre" could not fail for a long time to point a moral among a people so unused to violence and bloodshed. Paul Revere, who was one of the earliest of American engravers, published a quaint colored engraving of the scene in King street, which for a long time was widely circulated, though it has now become very scarce. Below the picture are the following verses, written in the rhymed tensyllable couplets which the eighteenth century was so fond of turning out by the yard: —

> "Unhappy Boston! see thy sons deplore
> Thy hallowed walks besmeared with guiltless gore,
> While faithless P———n and his savage bands
> With murderous rancour stretch their bloody hands,
> Like fierce barbarians grinning o'er their prey,
> Approve the carnage and enjoy the day.
>
> If scalding drops from rage, from anguish, wrung,
> If speechless sorrows labouring for a tongue,
> Or if a weeping world can aught appease
> The plaintive ghosts of victims such as these,
> The patriot's copious tears for each are shed,
> A glorious tribute which embalms the dead.
>
> But know! Fate summons to that awful goal,
> Where Justice strips the murderer of his soul;
> Should venal c———ts, the scandal of the land,
> Snatch the relentless villain from her hand,
> Keen execrations on this plate inscribed
> Shall reach a Judge who never can be bribed."

These last lines give expression to the feelings of those who condemned the verdict of the court, and they show how intense was the indignation over the bloodshed and the sympathy for the victims. The self-restraint shown by the people, while under the influence of such feelings, is in the highest degree creditable to Boston; and the moral lessons of the story are such as ought never to be forgotten. Adams and Warren, and their patriot friends, were right in deciding that the fatal 5th of March should be solemnly commemorated each year by an oration to be delivered in the Old South Meeting-house, and this custom was kept up until the recognition of American independence in 1783, when the day for the oration was changed to the 4th of July. At the very first annual March meeting after the massacre, it was proposed to erect a monument to commemorate it. The form of the proposal shows that the character of the event was understood by town-people at that time as I have endeavored to set it forth to-day. In dedicating this memorial on Boston Common after the lapse of more than a century, we are but performing an act of justice too long delayed. There let it stand for future generations to contemplate as a monument of the wickedness and folly of all attempts to employ brute force in compelling the obedience of the people to laws which they have had no voice in making.

LETTERS.

LETTERS.

The Citizens' Committee invited the Hon. FREDERICK DOUGLASS, the distinguished anti-slavery orator, to make an address in Faneuil Hall at the dedicatory exercises. Mr. Douglass wrote as follows, declining the invitation: —

LETTER FROM HON. FREDERICK DOUGLASS.

CEDAR HILL, ANACOSTIA, D.C., Oct. 5, 1888.

WILLIAM H. DUPREE, B. R. WILSON, E. M. CHAMBERLIN: —

GENTLEMEN, — Your respected letter informing me that a monument in commemoration of Crispus Attucks and others who fell in the massacre in State street, March 5, 1770, will be unveiled by the Commonwealth at 11 o'clock, Wednesday, November the 14th next, and also inviting me to deliver the oration on that occasion, came in my absence; otherwise you should have had an earlier answer. I exceedingly regret that my entire time and strength from now until the 6th of November, being pledged to the work of the National Republican Committee, with appointments already made, will prevent the acceptance of the invitation with which you have honored me. I shall probably come out of the campaign, as out of previous ones, with little nervous force left for immediate work of any kind, — certainly not enough to prepare an address suitable to an occasion so historic and grand as that proposed for the 14th of November.

I hardly need say that I am deeply sensible of the honor conferred upon me by your invitation, or that I am happy in the thought that the Commonwealth of Massachusetts is about to commemorate an act of heroism on the part of one of a race seldom credited with heroic qualities. I believe that Massachusetts is first in this recognition, as she has been first in much else that is noble, magnanimous, and brave. It was Massachusetts that, under the lead of her great war-governor, John A. Andrew, first armed and equipped two colored regiments for service against the late slave-holding rebellion. It was Massachusetts that, in those dark days, gave to the Senate Charles Sumner and Henry Wilson; and I do not forget that it was Massachusetts, by her advanced sentiments, made it comparatively safe for me to dwell within her borders when a fugitive, not from justice, but from slavery, fifty years ago. The recollection of these and other facts would strongly incline me to comply with your invitation but for the impossibility already mentioned. While, however, I cannot promise to deliver the oration, I do hope to be able to be present as an interested spectator of the ceremony of unveiling the proposed monument on the 14th of November next, and to listen to the oration in old Faneuil Hall, upon whose platform, in other days, the grandest words for freedom and patriotism found utterance, and have since gotten themselves incorporated in the laws, and measurably in the life, of the American people. It is meet that your grand old Commonwealth should take the lead in honoring the memory of patriots and heroes, of whatever race and color. She has this right by reason of eminent fitness. The tide of her civilization has alone risen to the level of this commemoration. Colored men fought with Perry on Lake Erie. Colored men fought at Red Bank in the Revolution. Colored men fought, and fought bravely, at New Orleans, under General Jackson. But no monument commemorates their services. I do not doubt, however, that the time will come when the colored man will have the same measure of justice accorded to him by others that Massachusetts now accords to Crispus Attucks, the hero of the State-street massacre in 1770.

Looking upon the magnificent monument erected in the city of Paris to the memory of Alexander Dumas, one of the most brilliant literary men of the whole constellation of French writers, I could not but credit Frenchmen with a higher degree of justice and impartiality to colored men than had yet been attained by my own countrymen. But when the monument to Crispus Attucks takes its place in Boston, this unfavorable comparison can no longer be made. In common with millions of my colored brethren all over our land, I rejoice and am exceeding glad that Boston is to have among her many other distinctions this noble concession to justice and patriotism in the person of one of a hitherto disparaged and despised people.

Very truly yours,

FREDERICK DOUGLASS.

LETTER FROM DR. HENRY I. BOWDITCH.

NOVEMBER 14, 1888.

MR. BUTLER R. WILSON: —

DEAR SIR, — I had received an official notice from the authorities at the State House, and an invitation to be present at the unveiling of the monument erected by the State to the martyrs to liberty, who fell in State street, March 5, 1770.

Your kind letter received last evening induces me to say to you that nothing but the present state of my health prevents me from accepting the invitation.

The two historical societies who have their headquarters in Boston have, by their committees, protested against the erection of a monument to commemorate a "*mob*," as they call the event in State street, and the just (as these historical gentlemen would say) death of "rioters." That "mob" was, according to Daniel Webster, the commencement of the war of the Revolution. I cannot see why we should have our "Minute Man" at Lexington, or our monuments at Concord and Bunker Hill, if this first clash of arms in State street — which some of the most prominent of the patriots of the Revolution celebrated year after year — cannot be justly commemorated.

Wishing you complete success, I remain,

Yours faithfully,

HENRY I. BOWDITCH.

LETTER FROM REV. PHILLIPS BROOKS, D.D.

223 CLARENDON STREET,
BOSTON, Nov. 5, 1888.

BUTLER R. WILSON, ESQ.: —

MY DEAR SIR, — I thank the committee for their invitation, and I should be very glad to do the duty which they ask of me, if it were possible. But I am very sorry to say that I cannot be at Faneuil Hall at the hour appointed for the dedication exercises.

I must therefore beg you to excuse me, and believe me,

Yours sincerely,

PHILLIPS BROOKS.

LETTER FROM REV. DAVID GREGG, D.D.

PARK STREET CHURCH,
BOSTON, MASS., Nov. 5, 1888.

MR. BUTLER R. WILSON: —

DEAR SIR, — I have an engagement in New York City for November 14, — a wedding. Were it not for this I would gladly comply with the request to close the Faneuil Hall exercises of that date with prayer. I would esteem it a great honor to be present at the dedication of the monument to Crispus Attucks.

Sincerely,

DAVID GREGG.

LETTER FROM HON. JOHN M. LANGSTON.

PETERSBURG, VA., Nov. 12, 1888.

HON. OLIVER AMES, *and others, Committee, etc., Boston, Mass.*: —

GENTLEMEN, — I have the honor to acknowledge the receipt of your invitation to attend the dedication, on the 14th inst., of the monument erected by your State to Attucks, Maverick, Caldwell,

Gray, and Carr. It would give me great pleasure to be present on such occasion. Thus, while I honored the heroic dead, I might have my soul inspired to new, earnest duty in behalf of the country and race, to promote whose interests and welfare they died. Pressing duties, however, detain me at home, and I am only able to tender you my thanks for the great service which the old Commonwealth of Massachusetts does humanity, — especially the negro race, — in the erection of a monument which shall tell to posterity how nobly these, her black revolutionary sons, among the very first to fall, March 5, 1770, to consecrate and make possible our national independence and free institutions, demeaned themselves in the face of danger and in the midst of fiery struggle.

Most respectfully and sincerely yours,

JOHN MERCER LANGSTON.

www.ingramcontent.com/pod-product-compliance
Lightning Source LLC
Chambersburg PA
CBHW031619170426
43195CB00037B/1273